SHIRLEY MACLAINE
& THE
NEW AGE
MOVEMENT

JAMES W. SIRE

D0754005

INTERVARSITY PRESS
DOWNERS GROVE, ILLINOIS 60515

Other Books by James W. Sire

The Universe Next Door: Revised (IVP)
How to Read Slowly (Harold Shaw)
Scripture Twisting (IVP)
Beginning with God (IVP)
Meeting Jesus (Harold Shaw)

©1988 by James W. Sire

InterVarsity Press is the book-publishing division of InterVarsity Christian Fellowship, a student movement active on campus at hundreds of universities, colleges and schools of nursing. For information about local and regional activities, write Public Relations Dept., InterVarsity Christian Fellowship, 6400 Schroeder Rd., P.O. Box 7895, Madison, WI 53707-7895.

Distributed in Canada through InterVarsity Press, 860 Denison St., Unit 3, Markham, Ontario L3R 4H1, Canada.

All Scripture quotations, unless otherwise indicated, are from the Holy Bible, New International Version. Copyright © 1973, 1978, International Bible Society. Used by permission of Zondervan Bible Publishers.

ISBN 0-8308-1106-0

Printed in the United States of America

13	12	11	10	9	8	7	6	5	4	3
97	96	95	94	93	92	91	90	89	88	

The place: Galisteo, New Mexico. The scene: the home of Chris Griscom, a woman who by means of acupuncture needles assists people with past-life recall. Shirley MacLaine, the well-known actress-dancer and star night-club performer, lies on a table, gold needles inserted just under her chin. In an experience that lasts for nearly five hours she envisions a scene she likens to a child's fairy tale.

> I saw myself with a herd of elephants in the bush jungles of the subcontinent of India. Green foliage surrounded clear green-blue water. It was a time period thousands of years ago. . . . I was living with the elephants. Immediately I understood that I could communicate with them telepathically. I was so well acquainted with their habits and feelings that on command they obeyed me. I was about twelve years old with dark eyes painted with tree bark that I had crushed, powdered, and mixed with water.[1]

As the vision or dream or imaginary experience or altered state of consciousness or head trip—one has difficulty in knowing what to call it—continues, MacLaine describes how she played games with the elephants.

"On my command they would pass me from one trunk to another while I laughed with delight." Totally carefree, she trusts them and they her. Wondering how she came to be in this situation, she is told that her father who had once befriended the elephants had died and the elephants, fearing for her life, had taken her away from the village to live with them.

While they occasionally return her to the village so she can enjoy human company, she lives most of her life with the elephants, learning to communicate telepathically with them "hundreds of miles away," taking care over their births, nursing them to health when they become ill and eventually becoming known as the "princess of the elephants." They in turn protect her.

One day, however, a friend in the village is murdered. Asana, MacLaine's name in this incarnation, cries for the first time and her hysterics baffle the elephants so much that the bull elephants almost destroy the whole village. Eventually, she and the female elephants calm the bull elephants and they merely surround the house of the man who had committed the murder and terrify him. From this the village learns that they had better keep the peace or be destroyed by the elephants, their "spiritual monitors."

When she asks what this vision means, she is told that the purpose of this incarnation and its recall is to help her relearn (1) the "lesson of democracy," (2) "the importance of understanding nature through animals" (*"They were completely without judgment* and an example of what humans needed to evolve toward") and (3) that, like elephants, humans never forget anything.[2]

The Attraction of New Age Spirituality
This section from *Dancing in the Light,* one of Mac-

Laine's five autobiographies, illustrates a host of characteristics that have drawn readers not only to her books but to her particular brand of spirituality.

One's first response, however, is a sense of wonder and even exasperation. We understand her longing for meaning and her desire for community with people, animals and the whole environment. But what is going on here? Can MacLaine be serious? Has she really lived an earlier life as Asana, "princess of the elephants"? If we say "Of course not," we are still left puzzled. How can she believe that she has lived such a life?

In any case the story illustrates a number of aspects of her religious convictions, all of them characteristic of New Age spirituality in general. These are attracting many readers and followers.

1. *The use of special techniques*—here it's acupuncture—*to achieve altered states of consciousness* in which one travels (in the mind—but nonetheless "really") to other "places" and special things are revealed.

2. *An interest in extraordinary human abilities.* Here it's mental telepathy and past-life recall. Elsewhere (throughout MacLaine's books) she talks about the channeling of wisdom and messages from spirit guides, some of whom are human beings at advanced stages of spiritual enlightenment (Tom McPherson, John of Zebedee), some of whom are extraterrestrials (Mayan).

3. *Reincarnation*—the idea that the soul lives and has already lived thousands of lives in previous ages. In one section of *Dancing in the Light* MacLaine gives a litany of some of her incarnations: a harem dancer, a Spanish infant wearing diamond earrings in a church, a monk meditating in a cave, a ballet dancer in Russia, a person involved with voodoo in Brazil, an Inca youth in Peru, a Mongolian nomad.[3]

4. *Karma*—what MacLaine calls "cosmic justice," the idea that we inevitably reap what we sow. Elsewhere MacLaine takes this further, declaring that we actually choose our own destinies, even the various incarnations we are in or have been in. We are in control of our own destinies, finally, because we are gods or "god."

5. *Solidarity, if not identity, with the animal realm.* All of reality is ultimately divine.

6. *The acquisition of power* (MacLaine becomes the savior and teacher of her village). In one incarnation MacLaine had mastered weather control.[4]

7. *The explicit notion of no judgment: ultimately there is no difference between good and evil.* MacLaine's own Higher Self tells her, "There is no judgment involved with life. There is only experience from incarnation to incarnation until the soul realizes its perfection and that it is total love."[5]

8. *A lack of concern for logical coherence.* Two morals of the story of her life as Asana simply do not follow from the story itself. First, there is no democracy in the story she tells. She and the elephants are in charge. Second, the animals are not "completely without judgment." The elephants—especially the males—were ready to take vengeance on the man who had killed MacLaine's (Asana's) friend.[6] Yet MacLaine does not question her Higher Self's incoherent explanation.

Dancer, Actress, New Age Whirling Dervish

Still we wonder. Who is Shirley MacLaine, anyway? Why should we believe her when she writes of all these wonders?

Shirley MacLaine Beaty (she dropped her final name as inappropriate for the stage) was born and raised in a middle-class family in Virginia; her younger brother is actor Warren Beatty (he apparently changed the spelling). Her first interest was dancing, and in 1954 she broke into the theatrical world as a chorus girl suddenly thrust into the limelight when the star of *Pajama Game* broke her ankle. After this debut she rose rapidly as a star herself, moving toward acting, first in Alfred Hitchcock's *The Trouble with Harry*. Though she calls this delightful film a failure, she has moved from success to success in singing, dancing and acting. She worked for McGovern in the 1972 presidential campaign and has been an active feminist. She has lived in Japan with her husband Steve (married in 1954 but soon separated and later divorced) and traveled around the world.

Her religious concerns emerged as she traveled the world over, notably Africa, the Himalayas of Bhutan and the Andes of Peru, looking for spiritual enlightenment. Recently she has held spiritual enlightenment seminars in such places as the ballroom of the New York Hilton (charging $300 a person) and has begun planning a retreat center for others seeking what she now feels she has found.

Her odyssey is recounted in *"Don't Fall Off the Mountain"* (where we can see the beginning stirrings of her longing for meaning in life), *You Can Get There from Here* (her least spiritual work) and the three more recent extremely popular books (all of which concentrate on spiritual matters).[7]

Certainly her most recent books have sold well.[8] By the fall of 1987, nearly three million copies of *Out on a Limb* were in print and *Dancing in the Light* had been on the *New York Times* bestseller list for thirty weeks. *It's All in the Playing* was then released in hardback with a first printing of 550,000 copies. Moreover, *Out on a Limb* was turned into a five-hour television miniseries and broadcast in prime time in early 1987 on the ABC network. "Though the ratings were low in TV terms," comments David Tuller in *Publishers Weekly,* "the numbers were huge for the publishing industry. . . . Sales of *Out on a Limb* and its sequel, *Dancing in the Light,* exploded, but the event provided a dramatic shot in the arm to the entire New Age publishing community."[9] She is currently working on a book tentatively titled *Going Within* that, she says, compiles "the techniques I have learned to work with over the years."[10]

Shirley MacLaine has in fact moved from dancer to actress to world traveler to New Age spiritual adviser, a sort of pop guru for the eighties. *Time* magazine in a cover story on Shirley MacLaine and the New Age movement called her "the New Age's reigning whirling dervish."[11] And Jon Klimo, psychologist and student of channeling, says, "Critics and fans alike concur that MacLaine has done more than any other single person in recent times to soften the ground for people to believe and participate in things they once avoided for fear of being thought 'flaky.' "[12] Even MacLaine sees herself at what she calls the "forefront of this movement."[13]

The Context for a New World View

Little of the above explanation, however, removes the puzzlement many people have when first reading her books. The issue still remains: why does Shirley MacLaine—one who otherwise seems so normal, so vibrant, so talented as actress and entertainer—believe all these things?

To put it succinctly, the primary reason that MacLaine and other devotees of the New Age have so little difficulty in launching into speculation about past lives, cosmic justice, mental telepathy and other such topics is that they have adopted a world view quite different from the traditional ones those in North America and Europe are familiar with. It is a blend of themes taken from three more common world views, two of which are characteristic of the Western world and one of which dominates the East. I am speaking of *theism, naturalism* and *pantheism.* And I must be more specific.

Theism. From the Middle Ages up to the eighteenth century in the West the dominant world view has been theism, in particular Christian theism. Though modern naturalism and Eastern views have emerged to challenge this view, it is still very much alive in the minds and hearts of Christians today. Like the other world views we will outline here, Christian theism is rich and complex, giving basic answers to the most fundamental questions human beings can ask: What is prime reality? What is the nature of external reality? What is a human being? How should we then live? We will sketch here only the barest outline of theism, just enough to help us understand the New Age alternative.[14]

First, Christian theism holds that the most fundamental of all beings is God. He is infinite and personal. All else derives from him but is not made out of his own substance. The opening sentence of the Bible sums it all up: "In the beginning God created the heavens and the earth" (Gen 1:1).

Human beings have great value and dignity because they are God's special creation, made in his image (Gen 1:26-27) and given dominion over the earth, not to exploit it but to cultivate it under the superintendence of God. Given the choice to obey or not to obey God, the first human pair disobeyed, believing the serpent in the Garden of Eden who told them that if they disobeyed they could "be like God" (Gen 3:4). From this initial choice came human alienation from God and, in fact, all the evils in the world from then till now.

Though separated from God's close fellowship and love, human beings are still important to God. From Genesis on, the Bible tells the story of God's action in history to bring his creation back to himself. It involves the formation of a people, the Jews, the revelation of God's intentions through prophets and eventually the coming of Jesus as God's own Son to die on the cross for the sins of humanity and to be raised from the dead to show that his death really was sufficient to restore a good relation between us and God. It entails as well the hope for Jesus' return to put a close on history as we have known it and to usher in a new age (though one very different from that envisioned by current New Age proponents).

In the Christian theist world view, it is God's own goodness that forms the basis of human goodness. It is God's own infinite intelligence that undergirds both the intelligence of human beings and the intelligibility of the cosmos. There are, therefore, both truth and falsity, good and evil, and God, not human beings, is the final judge of both.

For centuries in the West this was the reigning world view. Then in the Enlightenment of the late seventeenth and eighteenth centuries human reason—previously paired with biblical revelation as the accepted arbiter of truth—became recognized as the sole arbiter. God himself lost his personality in the minds of many people and eventually his existence as well. Naturalism was ushered in and has become a major if not dominant mindset of the nineteenth and twentieth centuries.

Naturalism. Naturalism is first and foremost what is

left over when God is removed from the picture. The cosmos still exists, but that is all that does. As astrophysicist Carl Sagan puts it, "The Cosmos is all that is or ever was or ever will be."[15]

Human beings are, therefore, only pieces of the cosmos—very complex pieces, to be sure, but having no relation to anything higher in intelligence or moral perception than themselves. They are their own arbiters of truth and morality. For various reasons (not the least of which is the memory of their being created in God's image), naturalists still generally hold to the dignity of individual human beings. Each person is valuable.

Because there is no God, of course, naturalists explain human evil and failure as a result of incomplete evolution or individual human choice or cultural formation. Solutions to human problems, if they exist, are solely in human hands. And because there is no supernatural realm, when a person dies he or she disappears. There is no personal afterlife of any kind. Death is extinction of the individual.

The bleakness of this view of human beings lost in a cosmos that did not intend to produce them and has no concern for them has long been recognized. The world, it is sometimes said, does not fit us. We long for an infinite ground for our human aspirations; we want to live beyond our appointed few years; we would like to find an overarching purpose to our lives, but we are offered none by naturalism. This has sent some into despair and others into giving up the search, ceasing to even ask the questions.

Others have thought that maybe the West went wrong a long time ago and so have turned to the East for a different view. Thus there has been a burst of interest in pantheism in the past fifty years.

Pantheism. Pantheism starts with a notion diametrically opposed to both naturalism and theism. For the pantheist, God and the cosmos are one.

The sentence that sums up the heart of pantheism is cryptic, but well worth the effort to solve: Atman is Brahman. Atman (the essence, the soul, of any person) is Brahman (the essence, the soul, of the whole cosmos).

What is a human being? That is, what is at the very core of each of us? Each person is the whole shooting match. Each person is (to put it boldly but accurately) God.

But we must define God in pantheistic terms. God is the one, infinite-impersonal, ultimate reality. That is, God is the cosmos. God is all that exists; nothing exists that is not God. If anything that is not God appears to exist, it is *maya,* illusion, and does not truly exist. In other words, anything that exists as a separate and distinct object—this chair, not that one; this rock, not that tree; me, not you—is an illusion. It is not our separateness that gives us reality, it is our oneness—the fact that we are Brahman and Brahman is One. Yes, Brahman is *the* One.

From this it follows that individuals are not of special value at all. What is important is the whole, the One. In the East, therefore, the truly spiritual person, like a drop of water falling into a bucket, loses his or her individual self by absorption into the whole. Likewise anything that keeps us from achieving unity—our desire for material things, for happiness, even for love and community with others—must be overcome. Thus there is an emphasis on various techniques—such as meditation—designed to help us get away from our individual selves and achieve unity with the One (Brahman) that we really are.

In most Eastern systems, however, individual souls do not adequately realize their divinity in one lifetime. Karma, the spiritual law of cause and effect, governs just what kind of life one will have in future incarnations. Some actions will cause one to move closer to realizing one's divinity, some further. In any case the ultimate goal is to cease being reincarnated and simply be at one with the One.

Because ultimate reality is One, without division, there is no ultimate good or evil, truth or falsity, illusion or reality. These distinctions are characteristic of our world in its disunified state and such distinctions are to be transcended.

If you were raised in the West and are hearing such a description of pantheism for the first time, do not be surprised if you are left confused and baffled by its lack of attractiveness. After all, who wants to lose themselves in an undifferentiated whole? We in the West cherish our individual personalities. We tend to think "things" are okay. In fact, we spend most of our time working to get them. We also like other individuals and feel human relations, like love, do not so much need transcending as they need to be realized in our lives.

That's where the New Age comes in. It takes the most attractive elements of all three world views, omits their hard elements and serves up a view of reality that caters to the modern age like grandmother's oatmeal used to calm the rumblings of my nightlong empty stomach.

Foundations of MacLaine's New Age World View

The New Age takes its view of ultimate reality from pantheism, including the notion of reincarnation. But it takes its view of the value of individual persons from Christian theism and naturalism.[16] In fact, it places even more emphasis on the individual than either.[17]

For Shirley MacLaine and New Agers in general all of reality is ultimately divine. Atman is Brahman is the ruling concept and yet the emphasis falls not on Brahman (the One) but on Atman (the individual souls). Each individual is God. In fact, it might be better to say that for the New Ager, Brahman is Atman. The self is the kingpin of reality. This theme threads its way through the last three of MacLaine's books, but seldom is more plainly expressed than in this:

> Regardless of how I looked at the riddle of life, it always came down to one thing: personal identity, personal reality. Having complete dominion and understanding of myself was the answer to harmony, balance, and peace. . . .
>
> I, now, on this street on this Earth, was experiencing only an aspect of what I really was. I was more than I perceived myself to be. And therein lay the grand truth.
>
> If I created my own reality, then—on some level and dimension I didn't understand—I had created everything I saw, heard, touched, smelled, tasted; everything I loved, hated, revered, abhorred; everything I responded to or that responded to me. Then, I created everything I knew. I was therefore responsible for all there was in my reality. If that was true than [sic] I *was* everything, as the ancient texts had taught. I was my own universe. Did that also mean I had created God and I had created life and death?[18]

What is interesting about this passage is how similar and yet how different it is from Eastern pantheist texts. Take the following from the Upanishads in which a father, a guru, teaches his son, a novice, that even a novice is ultimate reality:

"Bring me a fruit from this banyan tree."

"Here it is, father."

"Break it."

"It is broken, Sir."

"What do you see in it?"

"Very small seeds, Sir."

"Break one of them, my son."

"It is broken, Sir."

"What do you see in it?"

"Nothing at all, Sir."

Then his father spoke to him: "My son, from the very essence in the seed which you cannot see comes in truth this vast banyan tree.

"Believe me, my son, an invisible and subtle essence is the Spirit of the whole universe. That is Reality. That is Atman. THOU ART THAT."[19]

Notice the thrust of the dialog. The young boy is to think of himself as the "Spirit of the whole universe" but not as such in his individuality. It is not the boy who forms from himself the "invisible and subtle essence" of reality; it is the "invisible and subtle essence" that forms him. Individuality is lost in unity.

In contrast, Shirley MacLaine puts an emphasis on her own creative ability. This has much more the flavor of Western thought than Eastern, for in Eastern pantheism there is no creation as such; there is only emanation, the extending of the essence of reality throughout the whole of the universe. In the East this is not conceived of as a thoughtful process, for that which extends itself is not personal until it is extended. That is, personality is a form of illusion, not ultimately real.

For Shirley MacLaine the self, especially her self, is the really real. Notice how she continues her ruminations:

> Was this [taking responsibility for one's power] what was meant by the statement I AM THAT I AM?
>
> Was the search for God pointless because God was within me? Was God within each of us? Was self-search the only journey worth taking, because what we found, we would eventually realize, was our own creation anyway?[20]

MacLaine here appropriates to herself the self-designation of the God of Abraham, Isaac and Jacob as he spoke to Moses from the burning bush (Ex 3:14). There God tells Moses not to come any closer but to take off his sandals, "for the place where you are standing is holy ground" (Ex 3:5). God is emphasizing his distinction from Moses, equivalent to saying, "I'm God and you're not." MacLaine, on the other hand, equates herself with God, not Brahman (who emanates but does not create) but Yahweh, the God of the Jews and Christians (who creates but does not emanate). But according to the Bible it is the God of the Jews and Christians who has created her! She cannot be right that the Old Testament means what she means—that she or any human being has the power to create and to destroy, to imagine whatever one wants to and that's what will be.

This all seems so obvious to Jewish or Christian theists that their initial reaction is puzzlement or even shock. To do as MacLaine does here is to claim for oneself that which only belongs to God—his identity, his nature, his power. It is indeed to blaspheme. It is to believe the serpent in the Garden of Eden who when he tempted Eve told her, "You will be like God, knowing good and evil" (Gen 3:4). That was a lie.

Yet the claim is made boldly with no reserve. MacLaine calls it "*the* giant truth that one individual is his or her own best teacher, and that no other idol or false image should be worshipped or adored because the God we are all seeking lies inside one's self, not outside."[21]

Two Levels of Reality

For New Agers the world outside one's present consciousness has two dimensions, the visible and the invisible. Most of the time we are aware of only the visible world which we experience through five normal senses. But right next door is an invisible world whose character is quite different. We can enter into this world through special *doors of perception* (the term belongs to Aldous Huxley[22]) which we can learn to open through special techniques such as meditation, acupuncture and trance states.

Some people have more developed abilities in this area than others. MacLaine, for example, has consulted several channelers to contact entities in the invisible world. Keven Ryerson has put her in touch with two entities, one who calls himself Tom McPherson and claims to have once been a pickpocket in Elizabethan England and another named John of Zebedee who claims to have written the book of Revelation in the Bible (though what he says is quite unlike the content of that book).[23] And MacLaine herself regularly performs yoga meditation and has had an out-of-the-body experience triggered by staring at a candle flame while immersed in a spa in the Andes of Peru.[24] Also, as noted in the opening of this book, she has envisioned what she believes to be some of her former lives.[25]

When one enters the invisible world, the dimensions of space and time disappear.[26] It is there in this "invisible world" that, through the help of Chris Griscom's acupuncture needles, she meets in an altered state of consciousness her own Higher Self.

> I saw the form of a very tall, overpoweringly confi-
> dent, almost androgynous human being. . . . The
> energy of the form seemed more masculine than
> feminine to me. . . . It raised its arms in outstretched
> welcome. I got an Oriental feeling from it, more
> Oriental than Western. And I had the intuitive feel-
> ing that it was extremely protective, full of patience,
> yet capable of great wrath. It was simple, but so pow-
> erful that it seemed to "know" all there was to know.
> I was flabbergasted at what I saw, *and* what I felt
> about it.[27]

After asking it (she does not use a personal pronoun)
who it is, the being tells her, "I am your higher unlimited self." From that time on she takes it to be her main
guide and interpreter. It explains to her, for example,
the significance of her incarnation as the princess of
the elephants.[28]

Problems in Paradise: Beyond True and False

Even after grasping the major features of MacLaine's
fundamental view of reality, we are left with some major
questions.

First, how can MacLaine be both God and unaware
that she is God? That is what she says, as we have seen.
But it won't wash. If she is God now, she was God yesterday. If she knows now that she is God, she must have
known yesterday that she is God. If not, then we have
a God that grows in knowledge. But from whence does
God grow? If from himself or herself or itself, then he,
she or it was already that way. If from something else,
then God is not all there is and is thus not ultimate, not
God. For God there can be no growth in knowledge.

Second, how can both MacLaine and others be God?

Often MacLaine, for all her emphasis on herself, says that each of the rest of us is God too. But unless she is assuming the metaphysics of Eastern pantheism in which her soul is merged with the souls of all others so that there no distinction left, both she and others cannot be ultimate reality at the same time. MacLaine is too interested in her own individual self to adopt such a view. So what she says is simply self-contradictory.

Moreover, in reincarnation one loses (except in extraordinary, alternate states of consciousness) one's memory of earlier incarnations. Each incarnation seems at the time to be all there is to one's self; and each self is valuable. This seems self-contradictory, too. One cannot really be both a harem dancer and the princess of the elephants, having each self distinct and valuable and finally God, not at least without a merging in which the individual persons are lost.

MacLaine herself has puzzled over such questions. When her Higher Self says that there is no difference between her, her Higher Self and God, she asks, "Then how did we get separated?"

This is the great conundrum of any pantheistic system. If all reality used to be unified, then how did it ever become multiple? That is, if One is all there ultimately is, how did it ever become Two (and many more)? Here is her Higher Self's answer.

Basically we are [one great unified energy]. But individual souls became separated from the higher vibration in the process of creating various life forms. Seduced by the beauty of their own creations they became entrapped in the physical, losing their connection with Divine Light. The panic was so severe that it created a battlefield known to you now as good and evil. Karma, that is, cause and effect, came into being as a path, a means, a method, to eventually eliminate the artificial concepts of good and evil.[29]

This answer is, of course, not satisfactory. If higher being (the "higher vibration") becomes confused by its own actions, why should anyone want to become reunited with it? This kind of ultimate reality constitutes an exceptionally weak divinity. MacLaine's spirituality seems to be more a counsel of despair than an offer of hope. MacLaine, however, draws no such conclusions.

Third, why should any of us believe what she tells us about herself, God and the cosmos? Her views are based on (1) what she has been told by various spiritual teachers and voices coming through channelers claiming to be from other times and places (including extraterrestrial), (2) what she has experienced herself in altered states of consciousness and (3) what she has read in occult and other religious writings. She, of course, has ultimate responsibility for what she believes and undoubtedly feels that she has sufficient reasons. But do we?

Not really. For one thing, what is communicated through channeling is uncheckable. Was there ever a Tom McPherson? Is the voice through Kevin Ryerson his? Is what the voice says true? There is simply no way to know. Certainly there was a John of Zebedee who may well have written the book of Revelation in the Bible. But what Ryerson's John of Zebedee says is so unlike what is in that book or any of the others he is said to have written (the Gospel of John, the three letters of John) that his identity is more than suspect.

Moreover, MacLaine's own experiences are hers alone. The possibility of self-deception, let alone demonic deception, given the circumstances under which they took place, is clearly present. We too might have such experiences if we followed her lead, but these experiences might well be pure fantasy.

And finally, when it comes to trusting her reading of the spiritual classics, we have good reason to doubt. The following is typical of her approach. Reflecting on how she was beginning to get in touch with her "unlimited soul," she writes:

> The teachings of the Bible, the Mahabharata, the Koran, and all the other spiritual books that I had tried to understand flooded back to me: *The Kingdom of Heaven is within you. Know thyself and that will set you free; to thine own self be true; to know self is to know all; know that you are God; know that you are the universe. . . .*[30]

This melange of sayings combines phrases from many sources: *The Kingdom of Heaven is within you* is probably a misquotation of Luke 17:21 where Jesus says (as translated in the King James Version), "The kingdom of *God* is within you" (this verse is more accurately translated as "The kingdom of God is *among* you [plural]," or "*in the midst* of you [plural]," emphasizing the communal nature of God's reign among his people); *Know thyself* is from the Delphic Oracle and is quoted by Socrates; *that will set you free* are the words of Jesus in John 8:32 attached to the idea of following Jesus, a very different notion from "know thyself"; *to thine own self be true* are the words of Polonius, the old fool in Shakespeare's *Hamlet; know that you are God* seems to reflect Psalm 46:10 in which Jehovah is quoted as saying, "Be still and know that I am God," a quite opposite notion; *to know self is to know all* is a common idea in MacLaine and in Hinduism but its meaning is different in each; *know that you are the universe* is an idea common in Eastern pantheism but not in the West.

After quoting these lines, MacLaine adds that "the spiritual masters had all said the same thing. They had each taught that the soul is eternal. They had each alluded to having lived many times before, even Christ said: 'I came before, but you did not recognize me.' They had each taught that the purpose of life was to work one's way back to the Divine Source of which we were all a part." First, the spiritual masters often disagree on many important matters, including whether the soul is reincarnated. Second, MacLaine does not give the source of her quotation from Christ and I am unaware of it anywhere in the Bible, though it might be found in some ancient or recent gnostic text. In any case, nothing Jesus says there points to reincarnation or to the notion that we are to work our way back to the Divine Source. Finally, according to the Bible, we are not a part of that source but a creation of that Source. This is only one instance of MacLaine's frequent distortion or misunderstanding of religious texts.[31]

The point is that many of MacLaine's sources cannot be checked, and those that can be do not pan out. There is, therefore, little reason to believe her when she talks of spiritual matters.

Lifestyle and Ethics: Beyond Good and Evil

Shirley MacLaine does not have any clear ethical "teachings" as such. She seems rather to take normal, American middle-class values as a given: hard work, a good income, nice things, a beach house, freedom to travel and to entertain and be entertained. On most ethical and political issues she is "liberal": pro-choice on abortion, an advocate of feminist causes, and was an active worker in George McGovern's campaign for president and supporter of his agenda.

Her views on marriage and sex are quintessentially modern. She was married young, but soon began living apart from her husband and then was divorced. She has had several lovers, one live-in (a Russian film director), one furtive (a British politician).[32] She seems to enter all of these relationships with a certain gusto but without either a sense of long-range commitment or of much sorrow or guilt as relationships are ended.

In any case, she never argues for any of these views, just assumes them and assumes that her readers, if they are intelligent at all, will agree with most of them.

The central characteristic about her values, however, is that they are of her own making. She is, after all, whatever there is that passes for God in this cosmos. Her ethics are based on metaphysics. Since she is God, she is in charge.

> I could legitimately say that I created the Statue of Liberty, chocolate chip cookies, the Beatles, terrorism, and the Vietnam War. . . . And if [people] reacted to world events, then I was creating them to react so I would have someone to interact with, thereby enabling myself to know me better.[33]

She then takes as her New Year's resolution "to improve myself—which would in turn improve the world I lived in."

Her friends to whom she told these things "looked scandalized" and they objected that she had "gone too far." But then MacLaine realized that she was creating them to object, that they were characters in her play. Eventually her friends challenged her that if what she was saying were true, then wouldn't all her actions necessarily be selfish, that in truth she did nothing for others?

And the answer is, essentially, yes. If I fed a starving

child, and I was honest about my motivation, I would have to say I did it for myself, because it made me feel better. Because the child was happier and more fulfilled, *I* would be. I was beginning to see that we each did whatever we did purely for self, and that was as it should be. Even if I had not created others in my reality and was therefore not responsible for them, I would feel responsible to my own feelings which desire to be positive and loving. Thus, in uplifting my own feelings I would uplift the feelings of my fellow human beings.

How do we change the world? By changing ourselves.

That was the gist of my New Year's resolution.[34]

An Ethic That Is No Ethic

Two rejoinders are in order. First, the basis of MacLaine's ethics is egoistic, solely related to MacLaine herself. There is no self-giving love here. It is hard to think that a person living only for herself could be what is normally thought of as good.

Second, the ethics themselves rest on a blatant and giant contradiction. On the one hand, if she is God, she can do anything she wants. There is no one to judge her. On the other hand, she stresses self-improvement. That is what her experiences with past-life recall are all about. She is learning that she has a lot to experience before she can become fully what she is—God. That is, she needs both (l) past lives of experience and (2) recall of these lives so that she can understand what is happening to her. But what can self-improvement mean to God?

This same issue was present in the illustration opening this book, the story of Shirley MacLaine as Asana, the princess of the elephants. The animals, she says using italics for emphasis, *"were completely without judgment* and an example of what humans needed to evolve toward in that respect."[35] But, surely, that is not the case with the elephants. They determined that the man who murdered MacLaine's friend was guilty and they terrorized him. They "understood who the culprit was" and "wanted revenge." Without the restraint of MacLaine and the female elephants, the whole village would have been destroyed.

Moreover, what would evolution itself mean without there being a judgment as to what was more or less developed, more or less good, more or less complete and so forth? One can't have it both ways: either we should learn to make no judgments and thereby have no way to distinguish between morally good and morally evil actions, between more and less evolved, or we should make these distinctions and thus imply by our distinguishing that there is a foundation that can justify them. MacLaine makes distinctions and judgments on every page of her books, apparently not recognizing the internal incoherence involved.

In short, MacLaine's ethics are both self-centered and centrally inconsistent. An ethic which deliberately obliterates the distinction between good and evil is no ethic at all.[36]

A Better Way

It seems clear that the system Shirley MacLaine is promoting is inadequate for the task of making sense out of life and giving us a way to live. A much better alternative has been with us for centuries.

It is intriguing, however, that when it burst on the scene in Israel two thousand years ago, it was also accompanied by signs and wonders, and announced by a person who claimed to be God. Jesus upset the people of his time too, for while he claimed to be the one fulfilling the prophecies of the Hebrew Scriptures, he did not do so in the way expected. Like Shirley Mac-Laine, he said things that completely exasperated his family, his neighbors, the religious authorities and many ordinary folk as well. But what he offered was new life, a way back to close personal relationship with God. He lived for his teachings and he died for them.

But then he did one thing no other human being has ever done. He predicted his resurrection from the dead and fulfilled that prediction. He was not reincarnated to return as someone else. The body that went into the grave was transformed but it was the same body. The evidence for his resurrection is public and convincing, being summed up in a passage written soon after his death and found in the writings of one of his early followers:

> For what I received I passed on to you as of first importance: that Christ died for our sins according to the Scriptures, that he was buried, that he was raised on the third day according to the Scriptures, and that he appeared to Peter, and then to the Twelve. After that, he appeared to James, then to all the apostles, and last of all he appeared to me also as to one abnormally born. (1 Cor 15:3-8)[37]

Jesus' resurrection stands as the best single reason why we should believe him when he speaks of spiritual things. But there are other reasons as well, not the least of which is the obvious quality of his teaching. Instead of laying a basis for any person thinking or doing whatever he or she wants, Jesus calls us to a life of self-sacrifice and service.

His ethics are God-centered and other-oriented. The greatest commandment of all, Jesus said, is " 'Hear, O Israel, the Lord our God, the Lord is one. Love the Lord your God with all your heart and with all your soul and with all your mind and with all your strength.' The second is this: 'Love your neighbor as yourself' " (Mk 12:29-31). And in parable after parable Jesus lifted up the dignity of people, especially those at the margins of normal society: the lame, the blind, the social outcasts. He had table fellowship with the dregs of society, for it was they who knew themselves as poor, oppressed and needy, who knew they were lost and without hope.

Those who would follow him he called to live like him. "If anyone would come after me, he must deny himself and take up his cross daily and follow me," he said. "For whoever wants to save his life will lose it, but whoever loses his life for me will save it" (Lk 9:23-24). There is in none of Jesus' teaching the notion that each person is God or that people can decide for themselves what is right or wrong. Rather he treated each person whom he met as made in the image of God but fallen from God and in need of reconciliation.

So Jesus came preaching that in him "the time has come. The kingdom of God is near. Repent and believe the good news!" (Mk 1:15). We are not to recall our lost godhood or realize our divinity, but rather acknowledge that we are not the people we ought to be, that we have missed God's perfect standards for our lives, and we are to believe that in Jesus, God has reconciled us to himself. Our task is simply to acknowledge our true situation before God, bow in thankfulness for what Jesus has done through his death and resurrection to bring us back to God and, through the power of the Holy Spirit, begin living like his children, taking on the values of the kingdom of God, imitating Christ.

Jesus recognized the longings of the Shirley Mac-Laines of his day—and all of us, really—and he spoke words of great kindness. "Come unto me, all you who are weary and burdened, and I will give you rest. Take my yoke upon you and learn from me, for I am gentle and humble in heart, and you will find rest for your souls. For my yoke is easy and my burden is light" (Mt 11:28-30).

There is inadequate space to develop further the Christian alternative to Shirley MacLaine and New Age thought. The New Testament and countless books such as John R. W. Stott's *Basic Christianity* or C. S. Lewis's *Mere Christianity* are readily available for any who wish to pursue the search.[38] Suffice it to say that it is a system of spiritual enlightenment that is both self-consistent and in accord with the way the world really is. I commend it to Shirley MacLaine and all readers of this pamphlet.

Notes

[1]This account occurs in Shirley MacLaine, *Dancing in the Light* (New York: Bantam, 1986), pp. 353-58.

[2]Ibid., p. 358.

[3]Ibid., pp. 366-71. For a Christian critique of the notion of reincarnation and karma see Mark C. Albrecht, *Reincarnation* (Downers Grove, Ill.: InterVarsity Press, 1982).

[4]MacLaine, *Dancing in the Light*, p. 317. And while making her television special of *Out on a Limb*, she claims to have stopped the raining at Machu Picchu just long enough for the filming *(It's All in the Playing* [New York: Bantam, 1987], pp. 278, 287-94).

[5]MacLaine, *Dancing in the Light*, p. 341; see also pp. 338, 342, 351, 363 and 364, where MacLaine or her Higher Self reiterates the rejection of any final distinction between good and evil.

[6]Ibid., p. 358.

[7]Shirley MacLaine, *"Don't Fall Off the Mountain"* (New York: Bantam, 1971; original edition Norton, 1970); *You Can Get There from Here* (New York: Bantam, 1976; original edition Norton, 1975).

[8]Shirley MacLaine, *Out on a Limb* (New York: Bantam, 1984; original edition Bantam, 1983); *Dancing in the Light* (New York: Bantam, 1986; original edition Bantam, 1985); *It's All in the Playing* (New York: Bantam, 1987).

[9]David Tuller, "New Age: An Old Subject Surges in the '80s," *Publishers Weekly* (September 25, 1987), p. 30. This issue features several articles on the publication and marketing of New Age books and includes an extensive publisher-by-publisher list of books being promoted by New Age publishers.

[10]Quoted by Allene Symons, "Inner Visions," *Publishers Weekly*, September 25, 1987, p. 75.

[11]"New Age Harmonies," *Time,* December 7, 1987, p. 63.

[12]Jon Klimo, *Channeling: Investigations on Receiving Information from Paranormal Sources* (Los Angeles: Jeremy P. Tarcher, 1987), p. 42.

[13]MacLaine, *It's All in the Playing*, p. 172.

[14]I have described the three world views outlined here in much more detail in *The Universe Next Door*, 2d ed. (Downers Grove, Ill.: InterVarsity Press, 1988).

[15]Carl Sagan, *Cosmos* (New York: Random House, 1980), p. 4.

[16]For an extended panoramic view of New Age thought from the standpoint of the New Age itself see Marilyn Ferguson, *The Aquarian Conspiracy* (Los Angeles: J. P. Tarcher, 1980); and Fritjof Capra, *The Turning Point* (New York: Bantam, 1983; original edition Simon and Schuster, 1982). Excellent and extended Christian critiques of the New Age movement can be found in two books by Douglas R. Groothuis: *Unmasking the New Age* (Downers Grove, Ill.: InterVarsity Press, 1986); and *Confronting the New Age* (Downers Grove, Ill.: InterVarsity Press, 1988).

[17]See Robert Bellah et al., *Habits of the Heart* (San Francisco: Harper and Row, 1985) for a masterful study of individualism in both its Christian and naturalist dimensions.

[18]MacLaine, *It's All in the Playing,* pp. 191-92.

[19]From the Chandogya Upanishad, *The Upanishads,* trans. Juan Mascaro (Harmondsworth: Penguin, 1965), p. 117.

[20]MacLaine, *It's All in the Playing,* pp. 191-92.

[21]Ibid., p. 172.

[22]Aldous Huxley, *Doors of Perception* and *Heaven and Hell* (New York: Harper and Row, 1963).

[23]MacLaine, *Out on a Limb,* pp. 177-212 and passim.

[24]Ibid., 327-29.

[25]MacLaine, *Dancing in the Light,* pp. 366-71; see above, pp. 3-4.

[26]Ibid., p. 309.

[27]Ibid., pp. 334-35.

[28]See above, p. 4.

[29]MacLaine, *Dancing in the Light,* pp. 339-40.

[30]Ibid., p. 350.

[31]See also MacLaine, *Out on a Limb,* pp. 209, 211, 233, 239-40, 242-44; on p. 297 she inaccurately attributes "Know thyself" to Christ. Other instances of misinterpretation are found in *"Don't Fall Off the Mountain,"* p. 216; *Dancing in the Light,* pp. 114, 254-55; and *It's All in the Playing,* pp. 221-22. For a general study of misinterpretation of Scripture see my *Scripture Twisting* (Downers Grove, Ill.: InterVarsity Press, 1980).

[32]It is not clear just which details of her love affairs she describes in her books are fictional (designed to mask the identity of the other parties) and which are actual.

[33]MacLaine, *It's All in the Playing,* p. 174.

[34]Ibid., p. 174-75.

[35]MacLaine, *Dancing in the Light,* p. 358. See above, pp. 3-4.

[36]At least one reviewer of *It's All in the Playing,* Dennis Livingston, in *New Age Journal* (November/December, 1987, p. 79), has noted these problems: "I found the implications of her philosophy cruel and callous. . . . It all sounds like the perfect yuppie religion, a modern prime-time rerun of nineteenth-century Social Darwinism."

[37]The apostle Paul is quoting a creed that scholars generally agree dates to the A.D. 30s, as early as three to eight years from the date of Jesus' death. See Gary Habermas and Anthony Flew, *Did Jesus Rise from the Dead?* (San Francisco: Harper and Row, 1987), p. 23.

[38]John R. W. Stott, *Basic Christianity,* 2nd ed. (Downers Grove, Ill.: InterVarsity Press, 1971); C. S. Lewis, *Mere Christianity* (New York: Macmillan, 1952).

Actress, Dancer, Guru

Shirley MacLaine has had a distinguished career on stage and film, but her latest role is by far her most challenging. Spokesperson for a new religious movement sweeping America, MacLaine has written books, led seminars and even made a movie introducing New Age thought and practices to all who want to heed the call.

Using MacLaine as an example of New Age thinking, James Sire offers an incisive critique of the movement. He shows how it lacks logical consistency, how it differs from traditional Eastern thought and how it distorts Christianity.

James W. Sire, senior editor for InterVarsity Press, is the author of many books, including *Scripture Twisting* and *The Universe Next Door*.

ISBN 0-8308-1106-0

90000

9 780830 811069

P9-DVC-145